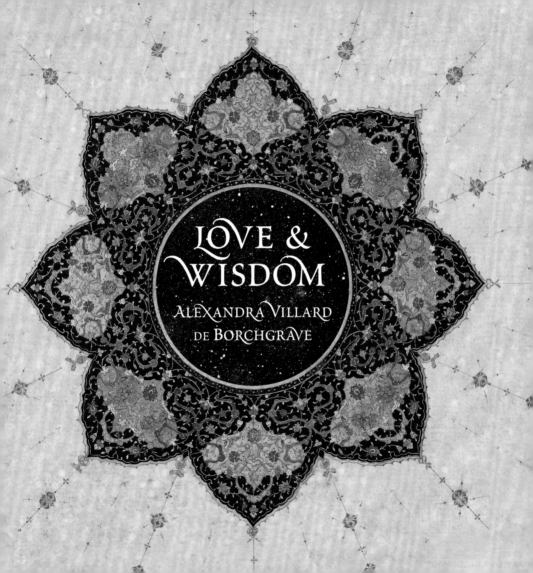

LOVE & WISDOM

ALEXANDRA VILLARD DE BORCHGRAVE

First published in 2018 by
GILES
An imprint of D Giles Limited
4 Crescent Stables, London SW15 2TN, UK
www.gilesltd.com

Creative Direction: Alexandra Villard de Borchgrave
Design: Henrique Siblesz, enlinea design
Photography of Illumination: Colleen Dugan, Freer|Sackler, Smithsonian Institution

Printed and bound in China.

10 9 8 7 6 5 4 3 2 1

British Library Cataloging-in-Publication Data
De Borchgrave, Alexandra Villard.
Love & Wisdom: 37 Timeless Reflections
Alexandra Villard de Borchgrave;
—1st ed.
A catalogue record for this book is available from the British Library

ISBN: 978-1-911282-29-7

DEDICATION

FOR Henri
And all in search of wisdom
to guide us and love to comfort us.

"If you keep your heart open
through everything,
your pain can become
your greatest ally
in your life's search
for love and wisdom"
~ Rumi

INTRODUCTION

My beloved late husband, Arnaud, was known as a brilliant thinker, and, in searching for a way forward after his death, I found myself drawn to wise sayings of ancient philosophers that were remarkably relevant to our lives today.

An extraordinary mathematician, Pythagoras believed the soul to be immortal, that it could rise to a union with the divine. He was fascinated by mysticism, finding power in certain symbols, such as the number seven connected to the seven "wandering stars" of the Moon, Mercury, Venus, the Sun, Mars, Jupiter, and Saturn. In studying his writings, I decided to divide "Love and Wisdom" into seven sections, Hope, Beauty, Forgiveness, Love, Kindness, Sorrow, and Wisdom and to fill each page with quotes from philosophers who lived more than a hundred years ago to reflect those categories.

In continuing to draw on the beauty of the past to connect with poignant words, I found inspiration once again in the magnificent collection of sixteenth century Illumination manuscripts at the Freer and Sackler Galleries of Art at the Smithsonian. I am deeply grateful to Director Julian Raby and Chief Curator Massumeh Farhad for their invaluable guidance in the choice of the images presented in this book.

In a new approach to my previous books, I incorporated contemporary images, many from National Geographic Creative, to serve as illustrative backdrops to the words.

Heraclitus said, "The sun is new each day." I hope we will use our time on earth wisely and that our troubled world will focus more on compassion, understanding, and peaceful coexistence, finding new ways to bind humanity together in love and wisdom.

~ Alexandra Villard de Borchgrave

CONTENTS

The Greeks were the first to think about the relationship
between color and emotion. The 37 timeless reflections in this
book have survived through space and time, offering inspiration.
They are arranged here through chapters in color associations.

PROLOGUE

Dwell on the beauty of life.

Watch the stars,
and see yourself
running with them.

~ Marcus Aurelius

HOPE

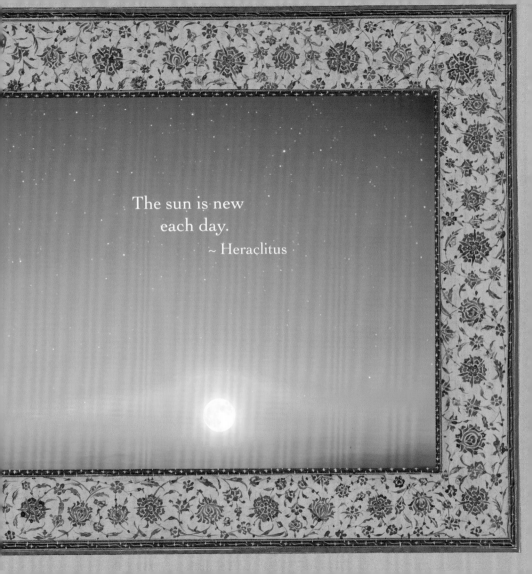

The sun is new
each day.

~ Heraclitus

Hope is patience
with the lamp lit.

~ Tertullian

Out beyond ideas of wrong-doing
and right-doing there is a field.
I'll meet you there.

~ Rumi

All the darkness in the world
cannot extinguish the light
of a single candle.
~ Saint Francis of Assisi

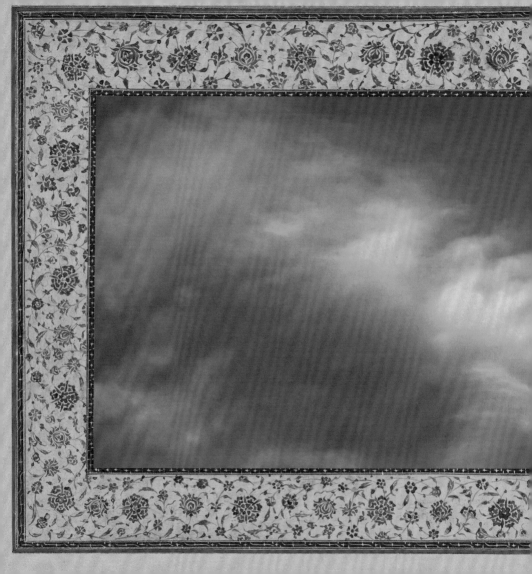

… hope
to the end…
~ Saint Peter

BEAUTY

Beauty is a
fragile gift.

~ Ovid

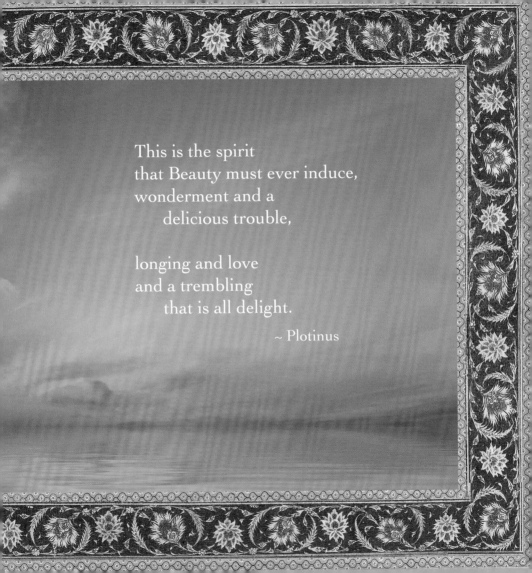

This is the spirit
that Beauty must ever induce,
wonderment and a
    delicious trouble,

longing and love
and a trembling
    that is all delight.

~ Plotinus

Everything has beauty,
but not everyone sees it.

~ Confucius

Since love grows within you,
so beauty grows.

For love
is the beauty of the soul.

~ Saint Augustine of Hippo

Everything… in any way beautiful
is beautiful in itself…

That which is really beautiful
has no need of anything…

Is… an emerald made worse than
it was, if it is not praised?

Or gold, ivory, purple,
a lyre,… a flower…?

~ Marcus Aurelius

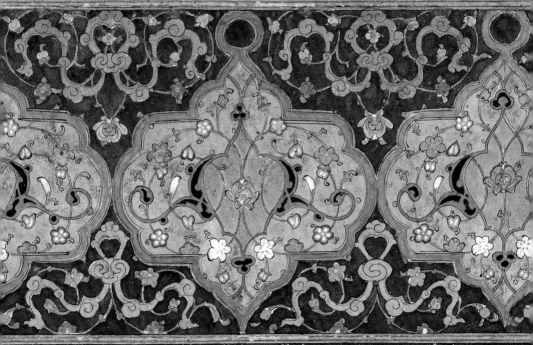

FORGIVENESS

He that cannot forgive others
breaks the bridge over which
he must pass himself,
for every man
hath need to be forgiven.

~ Edward Herbert
1st Baron Herbert of Cherbury

We pardon
as long as we love.
~ François VI, Duc de La Rochefoucauld

When you are ready to stand
in the presence of the Lord,
let your soul wear a garment
woven throughout from the cloth
of our forgiveness of others.
~ Saint John Climacus

Let us forgive each other —
only then will we live in peace.

~ Leo Tolstoy

To understand everything
is to forgive everything.

~ Lord Buddha

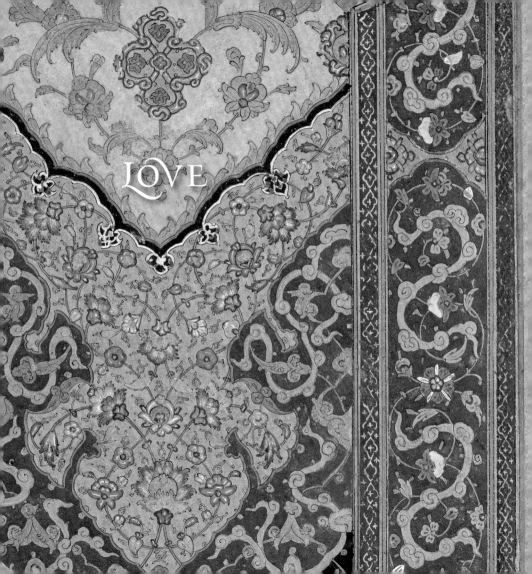

LOVE

There is love like a small lamp,
which goes out
when the oil is ended;
or like a stream which dries up
when it doesn't rain.

But there is a love
that is like a mighty spring
gushing up out of the earth;
it keeps flowing forever,
and is inexhaustible.

~ Isaac of Nineveh

Love conquers all things;
let us too
surrender to Love.

~ Virgil

Being deeply loved by someone
gives you strength,
while loving someone deeply
gives you courage.

~ Lao Tzu

How many gifts and graces
You have given me!
How many favors
You have fed me from Your hand!

I look for Your Love in all directions,
then, suddenly, its blessing
burns in me.

~ Rabia of Basra

Love all,
trust a few,
do wrong to none.
~ William Shakespeare

KINDNESS

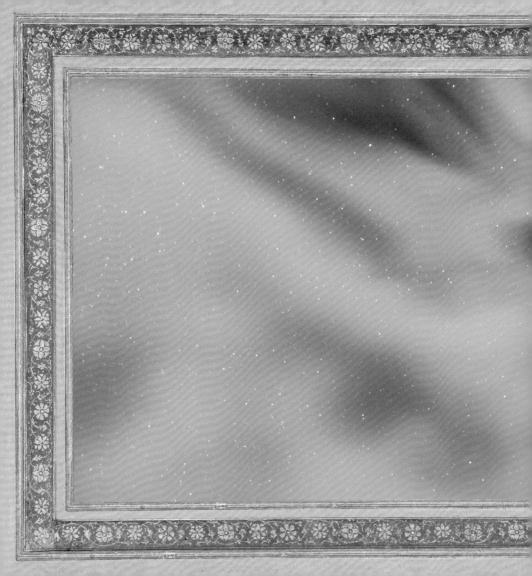

Be kind,
for everyone
you meet

is fighting
a hard battle.
~ Ian Maclaren

Always, whatever else you do, my heart,
Try to be kind, try to be true, my heart…

~ Jahan Malek Khatun

From kindness, hidden in hardness,
Turn not the face from hope…

~ Hafez

Your own soul is nourished
when you are kind;
it is destroyed
when you are cruel.

~ King Solomon

I shall light
a candle of understanding
in thine heart,

which shall not be put out.

~ The Apocrypha

SORROW

Here bring your wounded hearts,
here tell your anguish;
Earth has no sorrow that
Heaven cannot heal.

~ Sir Thomas More

The wound
is the place

where the Light
enters you.
~ Rumi

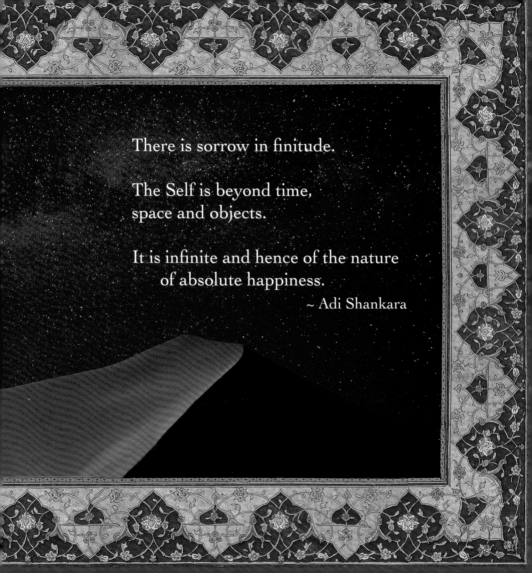

There is sorrow in finitude.

The Self is beyond time,
space and objects.

It is infinite and hence of the nature
of absolute happiness.

~ Adi Shankara

The heart itself is only a small vessel,
yet dragons are there, and lions;
there are poisonous beasts
and all the treasures of evil;
there are rough and uneven roads;
there are precipices;

but there, too, are God and the angels;
life is there, and the Kingdom;
there, too, is light, and there the apostles,
and heavenly cities,
and treasures of grace.
    All things lie within that little space.

~ Macarius the Great

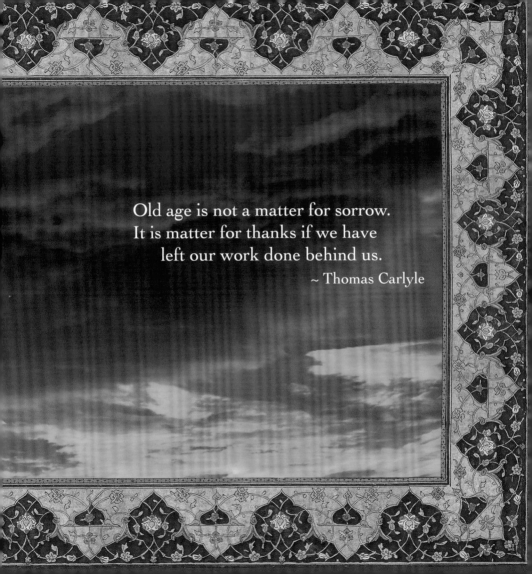

Old age is not a matter for sorrow.
It is matter for thanks if we have
left our work done behind us.

~ Thomas Carlyle

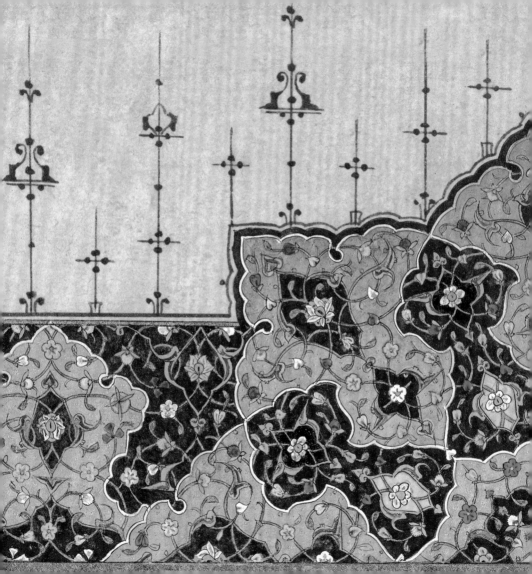

Wisdom

Like billowing clouds,
like the incessant gurgle
of the brook,

the longing of the spirit
can never be stilled.

~ Hildegard of Bingen

Waste not fresh tears
over old griefs.

~ Euripides

Truly, it is in darkness
that one finds the light,

so when we are in sorrow,
then this light
is nearest of all to us.

~ Meister Eckhart

Suffering becomes beautiful
when anyone bears great calamities
with cheerfulness,

not through insensibility
    but through greatness of mind.

~ Aristotle

All religions must be tolerated…
for every man
must get to heaven
in his own way.

~ Epictetus

EPILOGUE

What you leave behind
is not what is engraved
in stone monuments,

but what is woven
into the lives of others.

~ Pericles

INSPIRATION

We find inspiration from words, no matter when they were composed. Many quotes are common adaptations of the original. Included are brief descriptions of the authors cited.

THE APOCRYPHA (THE HIDDEN BOOKS)
Religious texts included in early Christian Bibles regarded as canonical only by Roman Catholics.

ARISTOTLE
384 BCE – 322 · Greek
Philosopher and scientist learned in botany, zoology, biology, physics, metaphysics, logic, ethics, psychology, poetry, theater, rhetoric, linguistics, politics and government. He was revered as the "First Teacher."

MARCUS AURELIUS
121 – 180 · Roman
Emperor, philosopher, prolific writer of *Meditations*, the most important source of Stoic philosophy and description of equanimity in conflict. Referenced from *Meditations by Marcus Aurelius*, Translated by George Long 1910

RABIA OF BASRA — KNOWN AS RABIA BASRI
714/718 – 801 · Iraqi
Muslim saint and Sufi mystic, she is considered to have been the most influential Sufi woman in Islamic history and was known for her concept of Divine love, her virtue and piety. Cited from *Souls on Fire, Selections from Eight Sufi Mystics*

HILDEGARD OF BINGEN
1098 – 1179 · German
Benedictine Abbess, poet, composer, and mystic visionary canonized in 2012 by Pope Benedict XVI. *Meditations with Hildegard of Bingen* edited by Gabriele Uhlein published by Inner Traditions International and Bear & Company, ©1983. All rights reserved. www.Innertraditions.com Reprinted with permission of publisher.

LORD BUDDHA
c.563/480 BCE – c.483/400
Siddhārtha Gautama, the founder of Buddhism and teacher in the pursuit of wisdom, loving-kindness, and compassion.

THOMAS CARLYLE
1795 – 1881 · British
Historian, mathematician, and essayist born in Scotland whose famous work, *The French Revolution*, was his greatest achievement.

CONFUCIUS
551 BCE – 479 · Chinese
Teacher, editor, politician, and philosopher who encouraged justice, sincerity, the veneration of elders, and strong family loyalty.

**JOHANNES ECKHART —
KNOWN AS MEISTER
ECKHART**
1260 – 1328 · German
Philosopher, theologian,
and renowned mystic who
joined the Roman Catholic
Dominican Order at 15
and later wrote the famous
Book of Divine Consolation.

EPICTETUS
c.55 – 135 · Greek
Stoic philosopher born a
slave in Rome, freed after
Nero's death, who taught
dispassionate acceptance
of external events
beyond control.

EURIPIDES
484 BCE – 406 · Greek
Dramatist, author of
notable works, including
Medea and *Electra*, who
had a profound influence
on such writers as
Shakespeare and Racine.

**KHWĀJA SHAMS-UD-DĪN
MUḤAMMAD ḤĀFEẒ-E SHĪRĀZĪ
— KNOWN AS HAFEZ**
1325 – 1390 · Persian
Considered one of the finest
lyric poets of Persia whose
poems expressed the ecstasy
of divine love.
Cited from *The Divan*, translated
by H. Wilberforce Clarke 1891

HERACLITUS
c.540 BCE – c.480 · Greek
Aristocrat known as the
"Weeping Philosopher" who
led a lonely life preaching
the need for people to live
in social harmony.

**EDWARD HERBERT, 1ST BARON
HERBERT OF CHERBURY**
1583 – 1648 · British
Diplomat, soldier, historian,
and philosopher. He served as
ambassador to Paris and wrote
the first English metaphysical
treatise *De Veritate*.
Cited from *The Autobiography of
Edward, Lord Herbert of Cherbury*
by Sidney Lee 1886

JAHAN-MALEK KHATUN
724/1324 – 784/1382 · Persian
Injuid princess and poet
known for her ghazals,
rhyming poems expressing
pain of loss and the beauty
of love despite the pain.
"Always, whatever else you
do my heart" by Jahan Malek
Khatun translated by Dick
Davis, in *Faces of Love: Hafez
and the Poets of Shiraz*, ©2012
www.mage.com

LAO TZU (LAOZI)
c.6th century BCE · Chinese
Philosopher and writer,
reputedly the founder
of Taoism, emphasizing
compassion, frugality,
and humility.

**FRANÇOIS VI, DUC DE
LA ROCHEFOUCAULD**
1613 – 1680 · French
Nobleman and writer who
served in the military. He
was famous for his *Maximes*
containing epigrams on
human nature, including
pride and self-love.

MACARIUS THE GREAT
300 – 390 · Egyptian
Christian saint known for
his wisdom and abstinence
from worldly pleasures in
favor of spiritual goals.
Translation cited from
*The Book of Mystical Chapters:
Meditations on the Soul's Ascent*
with permission from the
Very Reverend John
Anthony McGuckin

JOHN WATSON —
KNOWN AS IAN MACLAREN
1850 – 1907 · Scots
Presbyterian minister,
author, and theologian,
recently credited with the
famous quote "Be kind…"
originally attributed
to Plato.

SIR THOMAS MORE
1478 – 1535 · English
Humanist, lawyer,
philosopher, councillor to
Henry VIII, and author
of *Utopia*. Against the
Protestant Reformation.
Executed for refusing to
take the Oath of Supremacy.

ISAAC OF NINEVEH
c.613 – c.700 · Syrian
Christian mystical saint
known for his spiritual
discourses on love, faith and
kindness who advocated
universal reconciliation.
Translation cited in *The
Enlightened Mind: An Anthology of
Sacred Prose* by Stephen Mitchell.
Harper Collins ©1991
www.harpercollins.com
Reprinted with permission
of publisher.

PUBLIUS OVIDIUS NASO —
KNOWN AS OVID
43 BCE – 17/18 CE · Roman
Poet most famous for his work
Metamorphoses, an important
source of classical mythology.

PERICLES
c.495 BCE – 429 · Greek
Statesman, orator, and general
who led Athens during the
"Age of Pericles," fostering
democracy, arts and literature,
and the beautification
of Athens.

PLOTINUS
c.204/5 – 270 · Greek
Philosopher and metaphysical
writer of the neo-Platonic
tradition who was born in
Egypt. He was best known
for three principles: the One,
the Intellect, and the Soul.
Cited from *The Six Enneads*
by Plotinus translated by
Stephen MacKenna and B.S. Page
1917 – 1930

PYTHAGORAS
c.570 BCE – c.500/490 · Greek
Mathematician who believed the
soul to be immortal. Fascinated
by mysticism, he found power
in symbols, such as the number
seven connected to the Moon,
Mercury, Venus, the Sun,
Mars, Jupiter, and Saturn.

**JALĀL AD-DĪN MUHAMMAD
RŪMĪ** — KNOWN AS RUMI
1207 – 1273 · Persian
Muslim jurist, Islamic scholar,
and Sufi mystic poet whose
main purpose was union
with the Beloved. His writings
promoted tolerance, goodness,
charity, and awareness
through love.

SAINT AUGUSTINE OF HIPPO
354 – 430 · **Roman**
Early Christian who became
Bishop of Hippo Regius in
North Africa
and recognized as a saint
in the Catholic Church.

SAINT FRANCIS OF ASSISI
1181/1182 – 1226 · **Italian**
Roman Catholic friar and
preacher, canonized by
Pope Gregory IX. Patron
saint of Italy also known for
his patronage of animals.

SAINT JOHN CLIMACUS
c.579 – 649 · **Syrian**
Byzantine monk on
Mount Sinai, author of
The Ladder of Divine Ascent
who was revered as a saint.
Abbot of Raithu.
Translation cited from
The Book of Mystical Chapters:
Meditations on the Soul's Ascent
with permission from the
Very Reverend John
Anthony McGuckin

SAINT PETER
1 – 64/68 · **Galilean**
Fisherman, leader of the Twelve
Apostles of Jesus, ordained
by Jesus, First Bishop of Rome,
First Bishop of Antioch.

WILLIAM SHAKESPEARE
1564 – 1616 · **English**
Poet, actor, and playwright
considered the finest writer in
the English language of plays,
sonnets, and narrative poems.

ADI SHANKARA
788 – 820 · **Hindu**
Philosopher and theologian
who established the *Advaita*
Vedanta doctrine and explained
the existence of the Soul
in Hinduism.

KING SOLOMON
c.1010 BCE – 931 · **Israelite**
King of great wealth and wisdom
who also sinned. One of the 48
prophets according to the Talmud
and builder of the First Temple
in Jerusalem as recorded in
the Hebrew Bible.

TERTULLIAN
c.155 – c.240 · **Roman**
Early Christian author of
Berber origin from Carthage
in the Roman province of
Africa, he was called the
"father of Latin Christianity."

LEV NIKOLAYEVICH, GRAF
(COUNT) TOLSTOY —
KNOWN AS LEO TOLSTOY
1828 – 1910 · **Russian**
Writer whose famous novels
include *War and Peace* and
Anna Karenina, and who
became a Christian anarchist
and pacifist after a deep moral
crisis and spiritual awakening.

PUBLIUS VERGILIUS MARO —
KNOWN AS VIRGIL
70 – 19 BCE · **Roman**
Poet excelling in epic poetry
whose most famous works
in Latin include the *Eclogues*,
the *Georgics*, and the national
epic poem *Aeneid*.

Every effort has been made to obtain the necessary permissions with reference to copyright material, both
illustrative and quoted. We apologize for any omissions in this respect and will be pleased to make the
appropriate acknowledgments in any future edition.

ARTWORK

COVER

Mathnavi heading folio from the
Yusuf u Zulaykha, in the Haft Awrang (Seven thrones) by Jami (d.1492) Safavid period, 1557.
Purchase — Charles Lang Freer Endowment
F1946.12.84

COVER, ENDPAPERS, TITLE PAGE, & PROLOGUE — BACKDROPS

Getty Images, Sololos

TITLE PAGE

Folios from a Qur'an; Double-page frontispiece,
sura 1, verses 1–7 Safavid period, circa 1550.
Purchase — Smithsonian Unrestricted Trust
Funds, Smithsonian Collections Acquisition
Program, and Dr. Arthur M. Sackler S1986.82.1–2

HOPE

DIVIDER

Manuscript; Shahnama (Book of kings)
by Firdawsi; early 17th century. Gift of Charles
Lang Freer F1907.279

BORDER

Standing Figure Ascribed to Muhammadi
Safavid period, mid-16th century. Purchase —
Charles Lang Freer Endowment F1933.7

IMAGES

Getty Images, Misha Kaminsky
Getty Images, Mycola
Skip Brown/National Geographic
Getty Images, Ken Canning
Dreamstime, Carl Coffman

BEAUTY

DIVIDER

Mathnavi heading folio from the
Yusuf u Zulaykha, in the Haft Awrang (Seven
thrones) by Jami (d.1492) Safavid period, 1557.
Purchase — Charles Lang Freer Endowment
F1946.12.84

BORDER

Jahangir Entertains Shah Abbas from the
St. Petersburg Album. Mughal dynasty, Reign
of Jahangir, ca. 1620; Purchase — Charles Lang
Freer Endowment F1942.16a

IMAGES

Dreamstime, Volgariver
Getty Images, Goodze
Michael Melford/National Geographic
Robert Harding/National Geographic
Design Pics Inc/National Geographic

FORGIVENESS

DIVIDER

Folio from a Qur'an, sura 1:5–7; sura 2:1–8
circa 1550–1570. Purchase — Smithsonian
Unrestricted Trust Funds, Smithsonian
Collections Acquisition Program, and
Dr. Arthur M. Sackler S1986.84.2

BORDER

Folio from an unidentified text; recto:
inscription and seal; verso: Painting: A prince
enthroned and surrounded by attendants.
Timurid period, ca. 1425–1430. Purchase
— Smithsonian Unrestricted Trust Funds,
Smithsonian Collections Acquisition Program,
and Dr. Arthur M. Sackler S1986.142

IMAGES

Dreamstime, Jamen Percy
Stocktrek Images/National Geographic
Robert Harding/National Geographic
Getty Images, Julia Kuznetsova
Design Pics Inc/National Geographic

SORROW

Divider

Folio from a Qur'an, sura 1:6–7; sura 2:1–9, from a Qur'an (F1932.65) Safavid period, 1598 (1006 A.H.) Purchase — Charles Lang Freer Endowment F1932.68

Border

Mathnawi by Rumi (d.1273) Calligrapher: Sultan Ali b. Muhammad al-Mashhadi Safavid period (illumination and painting), 1458–1459 (863 A.H.). Purchase — Smithsonian Unrestricted Trust Funds, Smithsonian Collections Acquisition Program, and Dr. Arthur M. Sackler S1986.35

Images

Dreamstime, Elenatur
Getty Images, Leo Patrizi
Getty Images, Rattham
Getty Images, Idizimage
Getty Images, Ooyoo

WISDOM

Divider

Folio of Salaman and Absal from a Haft awrang (Seven thrones) by Jami (d. 1492) Safavid period, 986 H. (1560–1561). from a Qur'an, sura 1:6–7; sura 2:1–9, from a Qur'an (F1932.65) Safavid period, 1598 (1006 A.H.) Purchase — Charles Lang Freer Endowment F1946.12.182

Border

Portrait of Itimad Al-dawla Artist: Attributed to Balchand Mughal dynasty, Reign of Jahangir, early 17th century.) Purchase — Charles Lang Freer Endowment F1948.20

Images

Getty Images, Pixs4u
Getty Images, DWalker44
Getty Images, Mycola
Getty Images, Itsskin
Getty Images, Don Land

EPILOGUE

Getty Images, Rastan

ACKNOWLEDGMENTS

I would like to express my deepest gratitude to everyone at the Freer Gallery of Art and the Arthur M. Sackler Gallery at the Smithsonian Institution in Washington DC for the extraordinary generosity extended to me for over fifteen years through the kindness of Director Dr. Julian Raby. Starting in 2002, Debra Diamond, Curator of South and Southeast Asian Art, gave me permission to put my words inside their collection of 17th century Indian Mughal borders and Neil Greentree photographed the exquisite details.

I am most grateful to Dr. Raby for his enlightened thoughts in finding the right way forward with this new endeavor, *Love & Wisdom*, and I offer special thanks to Chief Curator Dr. Massumeh Farhad for lending me her warm encouragement and fine eye in determining the choice and flow of the Illumination artwork. In addition, I am very thankful to Cory Grace, Digital Asset Manager, for providing access to the vast museum archives, and to Colleen Dugan for her exceptionally skilled photography.

I am deeply indebted to attorney Jeffrey P. Cunard for all his invaluable and unfailing advice. I am very appreciative of Marjan Adib's helpful contributions to the collaboration with the museum, and to Sonja Potter also for her kind assistance on numerous occasions.

My heartfelt thanks go to Henrique Siblesz, the immensely talented designer who has worked by my side with me for the past ten years. I have dedicated this book to Henri, for I would never have been able to create my books without his marvelous graphic skills and steadfast dedication, starting with *Heavenly Order* in 2007, *Beloved Spirit* in 2011, *Healing Courage* in 2014, and *To Catch a Thought* in 2015.

On the night of September 11, 2001, as anguish hung in the air like a veil of tears, I began to pray for a way to bring some small measure of comfort and healing to the families who had suffered the most devastating loss of their loved ones. Then, on the first anniversary of that day of sorrow, as I watched the children call out their parents' names at Ground Zero with great courage, a space opened in my heart that made way for earnest verses about love, hope, and courage to flow out of me. The result was the publication of *Healing Light: Thirty Messages of Love, Hope and Courage* which was given as a gift to all the survivors families by John C. Whitehead, Chairman of the Lower Manhattan Development Corporation. I would like to thank Marta Hallett, at Glitterati Incorporated, for believing in my vision and publishing my works of poetry.

In 2010, I founded the Light of Healing Hope Foundation to comfort those who are suffering. I offer my fondest thanks to our President Katherine Wood, for all her caring support, our Vice President Sheila Stabile, Board Members, Advisory Board Members, accountant BJ Seebol, interns, volunteers, dear friends, and supporters who made it possible for us to deliver thousands of books to hospices and hospitals, including NIH, Johns Hopkins, and Walter Reed National Military Medical Center, to bring comfort to patients and their families who are experiencing the adversities of life.

I will forever be grateful to everyone who has believed in this journey of comfort and hope for those in need.

~ Alexandra Villard de Borchgrave

Alexandra Villard de Borchgrave has built a reputation as a photojournalist, author, poet, and philanthropist. Her photographs have appeared on the covers of internationally renowned publications, such as *Newsweek* and *Paris Match*.

She is the co-author of *Villard: The Life and Times of an American Titan* (Nan A. Talese/Doubleday), a biography of her great-grandfather, railroad magnate and financier Henry Villard, who masterminded the creation of General Electric. Alexandra de Borchgrave is also the author of *Healing Light: Thirty Messages of Love, Hope, and Courage; Heavenly Order: Twenty Five Meditations of Wisdom and Harmony; Beloved Spirit: Pathways to Love, Grace, and Mercy* (Glitterati Incorporated), and *To Catch A Thought: 50 Reflections for the Heart* (Light of Healing Hope Foundation).

Mrs. de Borchgrave founded a 501(c)(3) non-profit organization, the Light of Healing Hope Foundation, in 2010 with the mission of giving books as gifts to hospitals and hospices to bring comfort and healing to those in need.